My Trip to St. Helena Island

Discovering Gullah Geechee Culture

Written by C. M. White

Published by
Gullah Girl Publishing
www.helpingkidsrise.org • helpingkidsrise@gmail.com

For ACAK, LH, CH, AS

Always remember how amazing you are!

"Do your little bit of good where you are; it's those little bits of good put together that overwhelm the world." ~ *Desmond Tutu*

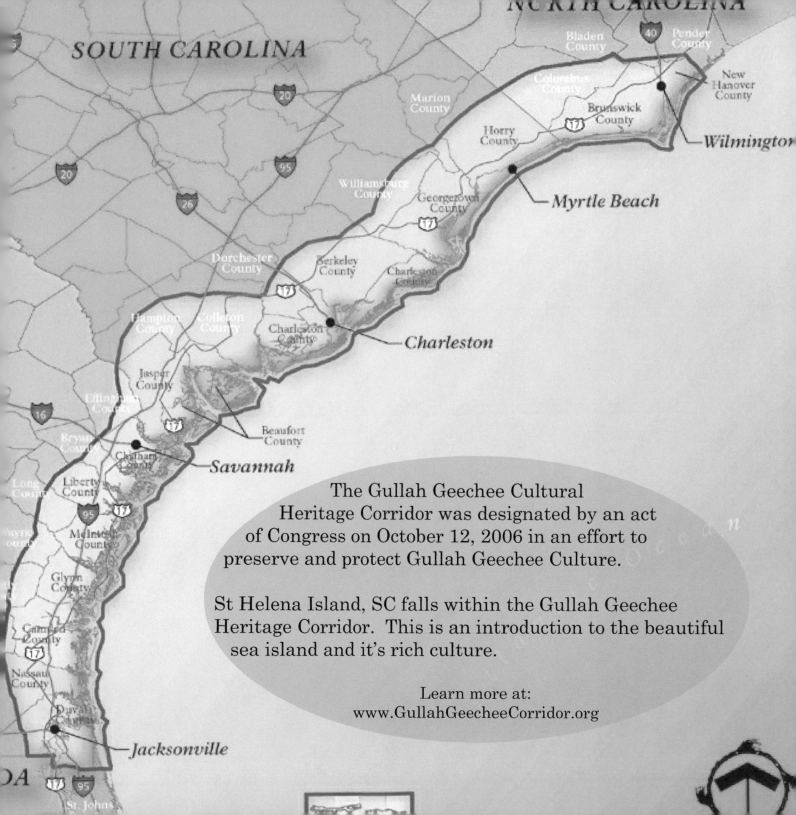

The Gullah Geechee Cultural Heritage Corridor was designated by an act of Congress on October 12, 2006 in an effort to preserve and protect Gullah Geechee Culture.

St Helena Island, SC falls within the Gullah Geechee Heritage Corridor. This is an introduction to the beautiful sea island and it's rich culture.

Learn more at:
www.GullahGeecheeCorridor.org

I arrived in Beaufort County early in the morning. St. Helena Island is located in Beaufort County.

The weather was perfect! The sun was shining and there was a cool breeze blowing.

The Woods Memorial Bridge is one of the bridges I had to cross to get to St. Helena Island. This bridge was featured in the movie, *Forrest Gump!*

St. Helena Island is a sea island. Sea islands are a chain of tidal and barrier islands on the Southeastern Atlantic Ocean coast of the United States.

I went to St. Helena Island to learn about the Gullah Geechee people. Gullah Geechee people are descendants of enslaved people from West Africa.

St Helena Island is full of Gullah Geechee culture. A lot of the language, foods, and traditions have been preserved over the years.

Beautiful rice canals built hundreds of years ago can still be seen along the coast today. Enslaved Gullah people designed and built the rice canals for growing valuable Carolina Gold rice.

I passed this interesting tree while sightseeing on St. Helena Island. The trees on the island grow, bend, and hang in mysterious looking ways.

My first stop on St. Helena Island was the historic Penn Center. It is the site of the former Penn School.

Penn School opened in 1862. It was one of the first schools for freed slaves in the South.

Penn School followed Booker T. Washington's model of industrial skills training. Gullah students learned farming, homemaking, and other skills useful for creating a successful life.

Penn School students also made beautiful sweetgrass baskets like this one. This handmade Gullah art began in West Africa. This art has been passed down from generation to generation.

The St. Helena Library has a beautiful room that's shaped like a sweetgrass basket. The library has won several awards for it's unique interior design.

The library's Gullah Geechee Room has lots of information about the culture. There are books about the art, music, food, and history of the Gullah Geechee people.

My next stop was this small Coffin Point Praise House. It was built by Gullah people around 1900. Can you believe it's still standing?

Praise Houses were built on or near the plantations where the Gullah people were enslaved. The Gullah people used praise houses for worshipping and for settling community disputes.

CHAPEL OF EASE

TO
ST. HELENA'S CHURCH.
BEAUFORT, S. C.
BUILT ABOUT 1740.
MADE A SEPARATE CHURCH AFTER
THE REVOLUTION.
BURNED BY FOREST FIRE
FEB. 22, 1886.
BEAUFORT COUNTY HISTORICAL SOCIETY

The Chapel of Ease is a spooky place to visit. It was built about 1740. The enslaved Gullah people built the Chapel of Ease out of tabby. The invention of tabby can be traced back to Africa.

To make tabby, the Gullah people crushed and burned oyster shells into a powder called lime. Next, they mixed the lime with water, broken oyster shells, and sand. Tabby making was a lot of hard work!

The Chapel of Ease burned in a forest fire in 1886. The roof is gone, but most of the walls are still standing.

There are lots of graves and spooky trees that surround these historic ruins.

Seafood is a big part of Gullah culture. Shrimping, fishing, and crabbing are major industries along the coast.

These blue crabs are fresh from the ocean. I think it's time to eat!

I ended my trip at the Gullah Grub Restaurant where I ate yummy food from the Gullah culture. Collard greens, gumbo, seafood, and okra are just a few Gullah favorites.

This trip taught me that Gullah culture is a big part of American culture. I can't wait to visit again to learn more about St. Helena Island and Gullah culture. If you get a chance, you should visit too!

Glossary

Carolina Gold Rice - *rice cultivated in the Lowcountry of South Carolina. One of the cash crops of during slavery.*

Cash Crop - *a crop that is grown to be sold. Major cash crops in the sea islands during slavery included indigo, cotton, and Carolina Gold rice.*

Culture - *a way of life. The characteristics and knowledge of a particular group of people, defined by everything from language, religion, cuisine, social habits, music and arts.*

Enslaved Person - *a person who is forced to work for another, usually under brutally harsh conditions.*

Gullah or Geechee - often *used interchangeably to describe the people, the language, and the culture.*

Gullah Geechee Cultural Heritage Corridor - *designated by an act of Congress on October 12, 2006 in an effort to preserve and protect Gullah Geechee culture. The corridor spans from the northeastern tip of Florida to the southeastern tip of North Carolina.*

Glossary

Gullah Geechee People - *African American descendants of enslaved people stolen from West Africa whose origins lie along the coast of South Carolina and Georgia, including the sea islands.*

Gullah Grub Restaurant- *Chef and owner Bill Green serves authentic Gullah cuisine such as seafood gumbo, shrimp and grits, and collard greens.*

Penn Center - *site of the former Penn School, which was founded in 1862, to educate newly freed African Americans. It was established on St. Helena Island as part of the Port Royal Experiment. Designated as a National Historic Landmark in 1974.*

Port Royal Experiment (1862) - *the American government's first attempt at educating African Americans who had been previously forbidden from being educated.*

Praise House - *enslaved people used these small frame houses as a place to meet and worship.*

Glossary

Rice Canals - *designed, built, and worked by enslaved Gullah people. Used to grow the valuable Carolina Gold rice that helped South Carolina plantation owners gain their wealth.*

Sweetgrass Basket - *handmade art brought to America by enslaved Africans. Gullah people continue to create this art today.*

St. Helena Island, SC - *located in Beaufort County. One of the largest sea islands in South Carolina.*

Tabby - *a type of concrete made by burning oyster shells to create lime, then mixing it with water, sand, ash and broken oyster shells.*

Woods Memorial Bridge - *began as the Lady's Island Bridge in 1959, then renamed the Woods Memorial Bridge when it was rebuilt in 1971.*

Photography by C. M. White
To purchase additional copies of this book visit *Amazon.com*
Inquiries: email *helpingkidsrise@gmail.com*

Get *FREE* parenting and education resources
@HelpingKidsRise

In Honor of Our Ancestors

We will always remember

"In all things, honor our mighty ancestors who sacrificed and endured so that we could exist today.
They are the light from which a new day descends."

CPSIA information can be obtained
at www.ICGtesting.com
Printed in the USA
LVHW071623250421
685525LV00001B/21

3 1901 04549 8690

* 9 7 8 0 9 9 6 7 5 4 0 1 9 *